SMART WOMAN'S GUIDE

THE MONEY BELIEF FORMULA:

MINDSET + BEHAVIOR

=

FINANCIAL SUCCESS

TRANSFORM YOUR HABITS AND WIN WITH WEALTH.

Written by

Susan M. Diamond

www.herfinanceclub.com

Copyright

 Copyright Susan M. Diamond 2021 - All rights reserved.

***

The content contained within this book may not be reproduced, duplicated, or transmitted without direct written permission from the author or the publisher.

Under no circumstances will any blame or legal responsibility be held against the publisher, or author, for any damages, reparation, or monetary loss due to the information contained within this book. Either directly or indirectly.

You are responsible for your own choices, actions, and results.

Legal Notice:

THE MONEY BELIEF FORMULA: MINDSET + BEHAVIOR =...

This book is copyright protected. This book is only for personal use. You cannot amend, distribute, sell, use, quote, or paraphrase any part, or the content within this book, without the consent of the author or publisher.

Disclaimer Notice:

Please note the information contained within this document is for educational and entertainment purposes only. All effort has been executed to present accurate, up-to-date, and reliable, complete information. No warranties of any kind are declared or implied. Readers acknowledge that the author is not engaging in the rendering of legal, financial, medical, or professional advice.

The content within this book has been derived from various sources. Please consult a licensed professional before attempting any techniques outlined in this book.

By reading this document, the reader agrees that under no circumstances is the author responsible for any losses, direct or indirect, which are incurred as a result of the use of the information contained within this document, including, but not limited to, — errors, omissions, or inaccuracies.

SUSAN M. DIAMOND

ISBN: 979-8-9854005-0-2 | E-book
Cover Design by Rihana Azam

For every sale of this book, Susan M. Diamond will donate to a US nonprofit, Working For Women, which collaborates with for-profit and nonprofit organizations across the country to help economically marginalized women achieve financial security. And the YWCA Ulster County, a nonprofit organization in her community, dedicated to eradicating racism and empowering women. Ten percent of the net proceeds will be split evenly between the two organizations. If you want to learn more, you can go to https://workingforwomen.org, htttps://ywcaulstercounty.org/.

This book is dedicated to all the amazing women in my life, especially my mother, Rosemary and my daughter Fallon, and the power of feminine energy and sisterhood.

I'm on a mission to spread the message that it's okay for women to talk about money.

My goal is to inspire ONE MILLION women to start a money conversation with their spouse, friends, or coworkers, removing barriers to discussing money and finances and aiding them in getting from where they are to where they want to be.

"The most difficult thing is the decision to act, the rest is merely tenacity.

-Amelia Earhart.

Just For You!

A FREE GIFT TO OUR READERS

What you need to uncover to stop sabotaging your financial health.

Ready to Understand Your Relationship With Money? This free DIY Money Story Guide will help you discover how to get started on your money story. Your past "money story" holds the secrets to your future financial well-being. Scan the QR code below to download:

Contents

Preface	XIII
Who Am I	XVII
Introduction	XXIII
Quote	XXXII
1. How Money Beliefs Affect You (exploring)	1
2. Money Behavior (reduce spending, increase earning)	15
3. Money Mindset (beliefs and behavior in action)	31
4. Money Belief Formula for Living a Rich Life Now!	45
5. Powerful Affirmations to Luck Into a Richer Soul and Happier Mindset	61
Quote	76

Conclusion	77
Resources	83
About The Author	87

Preface

When it comes to your money, do you ever find yourself thinking?

"I don't talk about my finances because it's considered socially unacceptable."

"I don't want anyone to think that I'm not smart with money."

"I don't want anyone to know that I am insecure with money."

"I don't want anyone to know that I am super stressed out about money."

"I'm okay with money and brushing it under the rug?"

Do you find it difficult to ask questions about financial products because it terrifies you? Do you worry in silence and assume there's no way for you to know enough on this subject?

I get it. I understand why you might think or feel this way!

Many of us get so caught up in what our mind tells us about money. Our belief that we aren't capable prevents us from achieving financial success. What matters more isn't what you know but the action you take when it comes to money.

The meaning of money is a mindset matter because it revolves around our beliefs and behaviors.

You might have been unconscious about how your behaviors create your results in the life you live.

You might have been living on autopilot without understanding the effects of your actions.

You might have been oblivious to how the world operates until now.

THE MONEY BELIEF FORMULA: MINDSET + BEHAVIOR =...

Raising your money consciousness is increasing your awareness and understanding of your money story. The story we tell ourselves about money shapes our beliefs, they, in turn, influence our behavior and, subsequently, our financial outcomes.

When you raise consciousness, everything changes.

Transforming your money mindset and believing you can is a critical piece of the puzzle. To successfully develop good habits with money, you need to practice self-discipline. Discipline is not always seen as a good thing, but it is really about reprogramming your mind and building self-control. Self-discipline means that we can be free from the expectations of others as well as our own weaknesses, fear, and doubts.

I help you break through the money blocks that are holding you back from realizing your full financial potential and reprogramming your mindset to win with wealth.

If you wish to permanently alter your outcomes with money, you must change your beliefs about money.

No amount of looking outside of yourself for the solution will work till you look inside yourself.

SUSAN M. DIAMOND

Who Am I

I love-as much as anything- helping women uncover their money mindset narratives and money blocks that are holding them back financially and how they can use this information to transform their results with money, build confidence, reduce stress, and live their best life.

This is what I do as a money coach.

The way I first got into finance was as a social worker, not as an economist or financial planner looking for patterns in people's attitudes toward and feelings about their personal finances. As I began to explore the unique challenges women face around finances, I discovered that many women out there wanted someone to talk to about these issues but considered the subject a social taboo.

Before launching the Herfinance Club earlier in 2021, I was Director of Women's Wealth & Philanthropy with a US Financial & Estate Planning Firm. I worked with women to help them accumulate and protect their wealth, and specialized in providing innovative solutions to planned giving, as well as founding the EmpowHer Community.

I have a master's degree in Social Work from Fordham University and was Certified by The Center for Financial Social Work as a Financial Coach, an approved program by the National Association of Social Workers. This was when I learned personal finance goes way beyond the dollars, cents, and budgets of traditional money management.

I've combined the most recent research and industry opinions into concepts and tools to help women break the taboo of money, feel more confident, and achieve better results with their money. By doing so, anyone can have financial success.

THE MONEY BELIEF FORMULA: MINDSET + BEHAVIOR =...

I wrote this book because money is so much more than the option to better our financial future. It has much more to do with our decisions and about it than simply what our "head knowledge" indicates.

I set out to bridge the divide between two critical issues that both the general public and the financial services industry tend to ignore:

- How we value money and our "Money-story" and
- How we relate to money

Before suggesting actionable solutions to improving financial wellness, we need to unpack some truths and realities to build a solid foundation. By doing so, anyone can change their money beliefs, rewrite their money story, and take control of their finances.

Money is a touchy subject; it is an emotional topic for many people. Money can be the source of intense stress or happiness, or it can lead to deep-seated feelings of shame and inadequacy.

Money issues are not just about what we have in our bank account; they're also about how we feel about money--and that's where problems start creeping in.

SUSAN M. DIAMOND

Money beliefs don't happen by accident; they take time and effort to develop--and once they do, they become self-fulfilling prophecies.

The Money Belief Formula is the key to understanding how habits influence our money mindset. Money decisions happen primarily through practice, not necessarily by chance. Instead, it happens because of what we do with our money--our behaviors and beliefs about it.

Money is the goal, and it's up to us how successful we want to be with money.

Fortunately, this book can help you learn more about your thinking processes. It will help you change your behaviors and beliefs and create habits that will help you win with wealth.

Once you are committed to mindset realization, we can work toward financial success.

I know it's not easy to believe that I care about your life and financial wellness wherever you are right now. But what we both want is the same: for your life to be better than before.

If any of this resonates, this book is for you!

THE MONEY BELIEF FORMULA: MINDSET + BEHAVIOR =...

Learn more about me on LinkedIn here https://www.linkedin.com/in/susanmdiamond/ or scan QR code.

Introduction

Do you feel like a Queen with all the money and resources available to you? Or are there days where stress has taken over, leaving everything in uncertainty?

Money is the root of all our woes; it can be a source of stress and fear. Or if used correctly, then money will free us to live more abundantly in this world!

The beliefs about money that we hold affect our relationships, how we feel about ourselves, and how we participate in life.

SUSAN M. DIAMOND

Our money mindset determines our personal beliefs, which are critical in creating wealth and financial success. It's the way we think about making money, saving money, spending money, and giving in our life.

Money is deeply personal, and it's how we feel about our financial situation that will dictate whether bad habits are created or good ones sustained. When we're feeling insecure with money in our lives, then the debt may become an easy way out because of its safety net; however, when one has plenty but still worries constantly over expenses like groceries every month- no matter if we've paid off all debts — these thoughts can lead them down destructive paths fast!

After years of thinking about money, it's time to give up the old stories and embrace a new perspective. So what have you been telling yourself?

You've got your template for how things should be: either there's not enough, or else all the good stuff is already yours! It doesn't matter if circumstances change because those perspectives are just that — templates - but they're way too limiting in their way as well- restricting our ability to experience life fully without being chained by these fixed frames.

THE MONEY BELIEF FORMULA: MINDSET + BEHAVIOR =...

People often have a scarcity mindset regarding money, believing that they're not good with finances, which many fear.

Here are some examples of a scarcity mindset:

- You have to work hard for money.
- I'm not smart enough to invest.
- Wealthy people are selfish and greedy.
- I don't deserve good things in life.
- Money is the root of all evil.

Now let's look at some examples of an abundant mindset:

- I can invest my money, and it will grow over time.
- I will be financially secure if I work hard and save.
- I control my money; it doesn't control me - I use it wisely.
- I deserve good things in life; I'm worthy of abundance!
- Money is a tool that can be used to serve others for the greater good.

A positive money mindset will lead you down better financial paths. In contrast, negative beliefs about money can hold you back from abundance.

SUSAN M. DIAMOND

Money is a symbol for value, power, security - whatever we consider valuable in our life - and it can also stand for feelings of abundance or lack thereof! We're after here the internal beliefs that have led us down these paths before - behaviors that don't serve us and the cycle of feeling not good enough because we're repeatedly sabotaging ourselves.

Our money mindset is the result of our prior life and childhood experiences (aka money story.) - Whether we grew up in an environment where there was never any shortage or if all the cashmere sweaters were gone by age six -.

It's about those verbal and nonverbal messages we picked up as a child - our parents arguing about money or that time your father told you, "Money doesn't grow on trees." It's about how comfortable we feel having money dates with our partner to discuss big life decisions. It's about cultivating our value as business or professional women when negotiating our salary or cost of service. It's about silencing our inner critic and counteracting, "I got this."

What's going on now can influence how well-off things seem later down this road for ourselves - both financially and emotionally.

THE MONEY BELIEF FORMULA: MINDSET + BEHAVIOR =...

The crucial thing to grasp is to understand one's mindset in the context of abundance vs. scarcity.

To build wealth, the first thing we must do is to take a pause and become aware of how our current money habits, perhaps, are standing between us and success, as well as the willingness to explore those limiting beliefs and shift them if we want to surpass our current financial situation.

Yes, there will always be unknowns in life; ups and downs are part of our existence. However, it is also true that no one can predict what will happen in even the very next hours or the next day, which makes it hard to predict what next week or next year will bring to us.

However, even though we can't control what is going on around us, we control the decisions we make today. It is precisely these choices that will determine where we land on the money game board in 5 years or even TEN!

To observe wealth-building behaviors take root, we've got to be willing and ready to change our money mindset to win at the money game and do things like earn more, save more, and invest more!

Money is just a tool and does not have any inherent value of its own. Money's worth depends on what we assign it to be. It has neither a mind of its own nor intrinsic value. Money is not emotional; WE ARE. Money cannot make decisions for us, but it can help us fulfill our dreams if applied correctly.

What comes first? The belief or the behavior?

The beliefs that we apply to our finances are directly influenced by our thoughts, which then impact the emotions that lead to money behaviors and habits and how they dictate what we do with the money we have.

It's all about changing what we believe and changing how we behave with money. The good news is that when it comes to behavior and mindset, there are no rules or laws-they can easily be changed because nothing is set in stone.

After understanding our money mindset, we can assess how our behavior is currently affecting it.

So, suppose we want to be more successful with money. In that case, we need first to understand that this does not mean changing what we do with our finances or even understanding more about it – although those things are important too. Instead, it means changing our behaviors and beliefs related to money and wealth to support the

THE MONEY BELIEF FORMULA: MINDSET + BEHAVIOR =...

positive financial outcome that we want to achieve in our life.

If we can change how we think about money, what it can do for us, and how to use it more wisely, then wealth becomes a reality.

As I mentioned to you earlier, my goal through this book is to give practical advice on how best for someone like yourself (someone who may be struggling financially) to identify possible toxic financial beliefs so we can start working together changing these negative thought patterns into something more positive-minded geared toward making your current financial situation more enjoyable instead!

Think of this book as the beginning of a new road in life that is filled with the wealth, joy, and success you have always dreamed of.

We will do our first step by bringing the light of consciousness to our thoughts about money and wealth, reflecting on them with an intention for change. A key component in this process is self-love; we must learn to love ourselves enough so that we don't rely only upon external validation when deciding on our finances or career path (this may put us on a precarious path).

SUSAN M. DIAMOND

Because, yes, purifying our money and wealth beliefs is an act of self-love that will improve our life significantly – if we have what it takes to succeed.

So, take my hand, and let's start this journey to a better life and a better you.

"The end goal: financial freedom!"

"There is nothing either good or bad, but thinking makes it so."

- Shakespeare

: Chapter One

How Money Beliefs Affect You (exploring)

Money is a much bigger part of our life than we realize.

We might know the pros and cons of money, but when it comes to how money affects us on an emotional level, things get murky pretty quickly.

Our money mindset is shaped by our personal beliefs, which influence our actions and, consequently, our financial outcomes. The beliefs you hold true are the most influential aspect of your mindset.

SUSAN M. DIAMOND

Money is a neutral energy that can become a complicated business, and that's because we have created or inherited so many Money Beliefs about it.

Money beliefs are what we tell ourselves about money--the limitations or possibilities regarding earning, spending, and saving money.

They are made up of three elements:

- Money Behaviors--How we act with money, what we do, and how often we do it.
- Money Thoughts--What we think and say about money.
- Money Feelings--How we feel and the emotions we have when it comes to money.

Self-limiting money beliefs- sometimes referred to as money blocks are underlying beliefs or fear that you hold on to subconsciously that can keep you financially stuck without you even being aware of it!

Limiting financial beliefs, money blocks, and emotions hitchhike on your money story, causing self-sabotaging behavior that keeps you in a financial rut (Examples include: avoiding paying your bills, eating out too

THE MONEY BELIEF FORMULA: MINDSET + BEHAVIOR =...

frequently, buying gifts you can't afford, living paycheck to paycheck, etc.)

Your money habits are directly tied to your money beliefs. Therefore, how you handle them can either help or hurt your financial situation.

Here's an example from a client of how self-limiting thoughts and feelings lead to self-sabotaging behavior: "When it comes to money, I'm a scaredy-cat." I'm overwhelmed and anxious about doing anything other than saving it. Then, some guy at Voya does something with my money that I'm not sure about. I know I should learn more and become more involved in investment and retirement planning. I'm so awful that I'm unable to read the statements. I just cut them up and assume everything is fine!!! "I wish they wouldn't send the statements at all."

When you ignore and avoid your money, you give away your control. Giving away your financial power leads to emotional and financial instability.

Additionally, money beliefs affect how happy or stressed we are about our financial situation. In the absence of self-confidence, we are less likely to take the required steps to improve our lives.

Neuroscientists have found that 90% of our decision-making is unconscious. This means that the beliefs and patterns in our unconscious mind determine what we want to do next.

The challenge, then, is how we can make our beliefs fully conscious to understand and recognize potential money blocks.

That said, how can we prepare ourselves mentally and emotionally for success?

The first step is awareness: Awareness of where our money habits currently stand and willingness to explore any limiting beliefs.

Money is money, and it makes no difference where it comes from; what matters more is how we think about our finances - this has a huge impact on whether or not we will be successful in our financial lives.

Awareness of Your Money Beliefs

This part will discuss how these thoughts – created, inherited, taught by parents, or teachers, etc. – affect how we relate to money and wealth.

Some of the most common money-limiting beliefs are listed here. Sure, there are many more of them, hidden

THE MONEY BELIEF FORMULA: MINDSET + BEHAVIOR =...

in our social, cultural, and religious customs, that might be around sabotaging you unconsciously.

What are your beliefs about money? Do you identify with any of these?

Money belief #1: Money will make me happy when I have enough of it

What it means: Money will make me happy when I can buy whatever I want without thinking twice about what else is going on in the world around us.

The truth about money belief: Money doesn't bring happiness, but a better life and time to spend with those you love does!

We don't need more money if we're spending our time working out how much joy there is in being alive - because that's priceless!

Money brings security and options for our future, so we are never stuck or tied down by anything financially again, leading to true freedom from fear.

Money belief #2: Money doesn't grow on trees

What it means: Money is finite, and we always have to work hard for what we want – there's not enough of it.

SUSAN M. DIAMOND

The truth about money belief: You're missing out on a lot if you think that way! Money can be made by smart investing or getting creative with your current resources.

Money belief #3: Money is the root of all evil

What it means: Money isn't good and should be avoided at any cost.

The truth about money belief: Money doesn't make us bad, but we can use our time wisely or mindlessly, which will lead to different outcomes in how financially abundant we are.

Despite popular belief, money is not a necessary evil, but it can be if we use it to harm others or ourselves. On the other hand, money is neutral and can be used positively to help us grow, build, or care for those around us.

Money belief #4: Money is what makes the world go 'round

What it means: Money is central to our lives, and we need it for everything.

The truth about money belief: Money isn't the most important thing, but it does have its place in life because, without enough money or resources, we cannot meet our basic needs.

THE MONEY BELIEF FORMULA: MINDSET + BEHAVIOR =...

Money is important and will continue to be in our lives for a long time, but it doesn't have the highest priority in life. You could prioritize many other things before money if they're more meaningful to you!

Money Belief #5: Money is protective, and I need it to be safe

What it means: Money is protection for your future, health, and happiness. Money makes sure you are always safe during any financial crisis or catastrophe that may come your way.

The truth about money belief: Money doesn't protect you from anything because it can be taken away instantly!

Having money isn't the answer to all of your problems, and it won't be there for you in all of your circumstances. Instead, money can be used to build secure and stable resources that can weather any financial storms that may come your way.

Money Belief #6: Money is not important

What it means: Money is not important, so much so that it doesn't have a place in my life. Money isn't given the respect or time it deserves because I think it's necessary for our happiness.

The truth about money belief: Money can be helpful when used correctly. You should treat your finances as an investment for your future rather than something frivolous. Money is important and deserves your time because it can provide you with financial stability, security, and the ability to make choices for yourself or others in your life.

Money Belief #7: Money was made to be spent

What it means: Money was made to spend because that's what we're supposed to do with money.

The truth about money belief: Money wasn't made just to buy stuff but rather as a resource that can help you get what you want and need. Money is meant for spending, saving, and investing. You can use money in many ways. We decide how we use our money because there are many options available.

Money belief #8: Money is hard to come by

What it means: Money is hard to find; you have to work for it and be super careful with it. Money is difficult to earn and not something that comes easily.

The truth about money belief: Money is a tool that can help us create lasting happiness rather than something

THE MONEY BELIEF FORMULA: MINDSET + BEHAVIOR =...

scarce and hard to come by. Money can always be found if we're looking or working towards a goal that will bring the financial stability important for our future!

Money Belief #9: You can't have everything in life

What it means: Many of us believe that there must be a trade-off if we get something good. Consider how absurd that sounds. It's as though people think the only way they can achieve happiness is by giving up everything else in life!

The truth about money belief: I have news for you: Yes, you can have everything you want in life. You just have to believe it and start creating it.

Your Return On Time Invested: Money Beliefs

As you can see, money has a meaning that is individual to everyone.

For some, money has the power to control their lives, while others choose to focus on wealth rather than fear, which will ultimately determine their financial future.

It's now time to consider your own money beliefs by asking yourself some important questions about what needs changing to create better habits with money moving forward.

Now grab a journal and write out Money Belief questions to ask yourself:

- Next, list your Money beliefs and the truth about each one.
- Finally, what are some habits that you can work on today?

By changing your money mindset, you can create better habits around thinking and acting with money.

THE MONEY BELIEF FORMULA: MINDSET + BEHAVIOR =...

However, be very aware that it takes time to change old patterns, so be patient but never stop trying to make changes that will positively impact your financial future!

Money isn't the root of all evil - WE are! The power to create wealth is within us.

Money doesn't have to be a source of stress for us - it can become our best friend or most trusted ally if we start thinking differently about money and its relation to our lives.

MY NOTES

MY NOTES

¨Wealth is largely the result of habit ¨

- John Jacob Astor

Chapter Two

Money Behavior (reduce spending, increase earning)

The vast majority of people I know are poor-minded. And you may ask: What does poor mind mean?

According to Jürgen Klaric in his book, Connect with Money, a fairly accurate definition of a poor-minded person would be the following: The poor mind only knows how to consume and spend; it is not programmed to save and invest.

Apart from that definition, the book explains that the poor mind is afraid and distrustful of money.

What determines whether we have a poor mind is the quality of our connection to money. It is something that depends on our values, principles, behaviors, and beliefs around money.

Raimón Samsó also explains it to us in his books. You will see statements like this in the Money Code: The solution to money problems is not in money but a different mindset.

As we may have learned from the last chapter, money beliefs are behind all the behavior related to our finances and wealth. Consequently, it is obvious that, if we encounter one or more limiting money beliefs in our system, these shaped the way we interacted with money all our life until now.

It is clear by now that our beliefs cause certain types of money behavior to play out in our life, and the effects our money behaviors have on our life can be uplifting, or they can be devastating.

We must accept and recognize that money is energy.

We can attract it or push it away.

What is the feeling we have towards money; do we think it is good or bad?

THE MONEY BELIEF FORMULA: MINDSET + BEHAVIOR =...

We label it good or bad according to what we have been taught, what we have heard, and what we have believed.

In the previous chapter, we learned what our beliefs are and reflected on them. We understand that money energy is neutral: it can be used for the good or the bad; it depends on the individuals.

Soon after, you realized that if money is neutral, I'm pretty sure this question crossed your mind: why have I not been able to accumulate wealth?

Perhaps, it's because your limiting money beliefs are deeply rooted in toxic money behaviors that unconsciously sabotage your path to wealth.

Of course, you have the power to change these toxic behaviors with money by doing one simple thing- stop engaging in negative behavior. But to do this, you need first to identify the negative behaviors and then challenge them.

Negative Money Behaviors

Money is a lot like food. Eating something that doesn't agree with our bodies will harm us. The same is true, if not doubly so for our finances.

Money can have a negative effect on us when it isn't handled properly, and the key to mastering money is getting into healthy money behaviors.

Toxic money behaviors are usually seen as bad habits. But, unfortunately, these are just the negative behaviors, often unconscious ones that hinder our wealth and success in life!

Of course, who doesn't want to be a millionaire? We all have this dream.

But not everyone knows what it takes or how they will achieve their goal of becoming rich and famous overnight with the touch of a button on some bizarre self-made machine that magically appears out of nowhere just when you need it most.

When the question was asked: What does it take to be a millionaire? Someone was ready to give that an answer, but it wasn't one that some were prepared to learn.

Thomas C. Corley, a financial advisor, has spent five years studying the behavior of different American millionaires and has compiled his findings in several books, including 'Change Your Habits, Change Your Life.'

THE MONEY BELIEF FORMULA: MINDSET + BEHAVIOR =...

Corley has interviewed 233 Americans who earn at least a $160,000 annual salary and have $3.2 million in savings and assets. He also interviewed 128 Americans who earn $35,000 or less and have no more than $5,000 in savings.

Through these conversations, he has been able to identify and analyze two types of behavior: those that help people build wealth and those that act oppositely.

Here are five toxic money behaviors that are driving us away from the wealth and success we want and deserve:

Toxic Trait #1: Making unnecessary expenses

It is impossible to get rich by spending more money than we earn. So don't buy a car or a house that will cost too much, and don't accumulate debts on a credit card.

"Ninety-five percent of the humblest people I've interviewed have failed to save, and most accumulated debt to maintain a lifestyle they couldn't afford," says Corley in his book.

True financial health comes from saving and investing a small portion of our income.

Toxic Trait #2: Maintaining unhealthy relationships

Sometimes it's hard to cut off relationships with certain people, especially those hurting us the most. But according to Corley, if we want to get rich, we must take this step.

In his study, he found that only 4% of the low-income Americans he interviewed were in relationships with successful-minded people.

"So much of your success depends on the people around you," he says. That is, we have to be surrounded by courageous, optimistic, curious, and generous people.

Toxic Trait #3: Falling into negative attitudes and thinking

"I'm not smart enough. It's not my fault; it's not up to me. Life is cruel."

According to Corley, these are the most typical negative thoughts. A pessimistic attitude will ultimately hold back any of the actions we put in place.

"When you allow pessimism to control your thoughts, you are programming your brain for failure," Corley clarifies in his book. "With a negative attitude, it will be impossible for your savings and assets to end up growing."

Toxic Trait #4: Unhealthy habits

THE MONEY BELIEF FORMULA: MINDSET + BEHAVIOR =...

Excessive alcohol consumption, a sedentary lifestyle, and an unhealthy diet are factors that end up pushing us off the road to success.

"Poor health habits end up affecting behavior and decision making," Corley explains.

When we are unhealthy, we are tired, less productive, more stressed, and much more likely to get sick. So how can we focus on building our wealth if we struggle with these factors every day?

Toxic Trait #5: Failure to create a strategy and a life plan

"Ninety-five percent of the low-income people I've interviewed didn't have a life plan," Corley explains. "Without long-term goals, we are like leaves on a tree in autumn, falling and floating without knowing where to go."

To come up with a strategy, all we need is imagination and effort. What do we want to achieve, and where do we intend to be in 10, 15, or 20 years are the first questions we need to solve to achieve success, especially financial success.

Success can mean different things to different people. But you still want to get paid what you're worth, have the life you've always wanted, and make a difference in the world.

The lesson of the story is that when we address self-limiting beliefs, we will transform our thinking about money and adopt new and different behaviors to achieve our definition of success. And it is this new course of action that produces new results.

Your Return On Time Invested: Money Behaviors

Remember that our financial success is a journey, not a destination.

The key to making our finances work in our best interest is transforming any possible toxic money behaviors into positive ones that will lead to wealth and success.

So, we want to avoid falling for these toxic money traits? Well, don't worry! I've got a few simple exercises that will help. Here they are:

The best way to stop spending money, is to set up systems to make it harder.

#1 The 30-day rule

Are you thinking of buying a new iPhone even though your current phone is perfectly fine?

For a decision like this that will affect your budget for several weeks or months, I recommend applying the 30-day temporary rule.

That's right, put the money it would cost into a savings account for those 30 days, and think for 30 days about the pros and cons of your decision to buy.

How badly do I want/need this item (do any other options work well enough), does price matter as much now compared to six months from now- heck, even one year down the road will apply here! This forces you to think about the costs, your budget, and Return On Investment (ROI.)

Ask yourself after the 30 days if the pros outweigh the cons. If so, go ahead and splurge! Otherwise, leave that money in your account to contribute towards savings, investments, or your emergency fund.

What Are the Benefits of Using the 30-Day Rule?

It's one of those ingenious methods to save money that is really a win-win.

If you still want that item after 30 days, you've won since you've given yourself permission to acquire it.

You also win if you decide you no longer desire it because you've saved the cost of that item, which is now safely in your savings account.

Create points of friction when shopping.

#2 Waiting 24 hours

But now, what if you don't have 30 days to think about the outcome of a purchase?

Then, you have the 24-hour rule and the abandon your cart method.

While shopping online, leave things in your shopping cart and return in a day. For example, if you put it in your cart at 11 pm, make sure you're still happy with your decision at 10 am the next day. Did you know we get a big kick of dopamine when 'hunting' for items online? But we don't seem to experience the same purely-positive feelings after purchasing: which means that you might be able to satisfy whatever happy feelings you're craving simply by adding things to your cart and then (digitally) walking away.

If you're a shopaholic and you feel you have "extra money" that you can use, at least take one full day to weigh in if what you want to buy is necessary for you, if it would improve your quality of life in the long run and if it would help you to achieve your financial goals.

If you say yes to all of the above, then that's the way to go. If not, you should consider increasing your income by working extra jobs so you can afford to treat yourself.

#3 Save $1 for every $1

Finally, here's another method to save effectively.

Before you spend, do the exercise of calculating how much you need to save to replenish that amount. For example, if you set out to spend $20, ask yourself how I will save back this $20 during the month?

If your answer is no - you have no way to save that money back in the same month - this means you shouldn't be spending it in the first place.

MY NOTES

MY NOTES

"Financial independence is having choices based on what your heart desires rather than clinging to what society deems necessary."

- Herfinance Club

Chapter Three

Money Mindset (beliefs and behavior in action)

What kind of picture would you paint if you could?

Now, think about your picture of money.

How does it make you feel? How do you interact with money in this image or video that plays inside your mind when money comes up for discussion in real-time situations like work, family, and friends?

Our Money Mindset has a huge impact on the outcomes we achieve in our life because it is the engine that powers our success. Our thoughts and feelings drive our actions.

SUSAN M. DIAMOND

Our actions drive our results. The results we have with money drive the experiences and choices we have in life.

A Money Mindset is a combination of our Money Beliefs and Money Behaviors. It's our money personality; it's about how we think about money, how we react to money, and how we communicate about money.

Our beliefs cause us to take action or NOT. For example, do you spend every penny you make, do you have credit card debt, do you have a rainy-day fund in place, do you keep all your money in a savings account or under the mattress and avoid investing, do you invest 15% of your annual income?

How we handle our finances and our emotional attachment to money is influenced by our mindset. It drives how we make key financial decisions every day. To illustrate this point further, let's look at what we do when faced with an unexpected expense.

We have all heard the Money Mantra, "I don't have it in my budget. I can't afford it."

But how does our Money Mindset influence what we do when faced with an unexpected bill?

THE MONEY BELIEF FORMULA: MINDSET + BEHAVIOR =...

Do you turn to credit cards instead of cash because money is abundant and easily available for borrowing? Or are you more likely to make a Money Mantra statement like, "I don't have it in my budget. I can't afford it."

Are you financially literate? Do you know how much your rent or mortgage payment is each month and what percentage of your income goes towards living expenses? Or are you struggling with making ends meet every month and hoping that money will magically appear to cover your costs?

If you're still with me, I'm going to ask you a personal question:

What Money Mindset did you develop during childhood?

It all starts in our early years. The Money Mindset we form as young children is the foundation for how we handle money as adults.

Your mindset creates your beliefs and influences your behaviors, thoughts, and feelings about money, stemming from your money story.

Everyone has a money story — The secrets to your future financial well-being are hidden in your prior "money narrative." So how well do you understand yours?

Your financial narrative began at birth and progressed over days, weeks, months, and years. It's a personal story concerning money, and it drives your day-to-day interactions and relationship with money. It's your past decisions that have shaped who you are today. Do you think of your life as a story?

The money messages we received growing up from those closest to us, such as parents, grandparents, teachers, and peers - these experiences combined form our money story.

Did you experience your family living paycheck to paycheck, parents arguing about money, or were you privileged to afford whatever you wanted, or was talking about cash considered taboo?

When we begin to observe our behaviors, it's important to ask ourselves, do I want to be telling that story?

Is it empowering or disempowering? Inquiry can be quite liberating. This is the #1 path to freedom that money has to offer.

We need to understand our sentiments about money since past experiences, emotions/feelings, ideas, and beliefs will influence our actions - consciously and unconsciously.

THE MONEY BELIEF FORMULA: MINDSET + BEHAVIOR =...

One of the first things is to become conscious of our money story and study our mode of operation (MO).

Your life may have given you all the tools necessary for your money to work. Or it might have provided you with false beliefs that have inhibited your financial progress.

You may be feeling or thinking:

- Lost when it comes to personal finance.
- Shame about where you are in your money life because you're:
- Still paying off loans.
- Surviving from one paycheck to the next.
- Spending more than your lifestyle and income can support.
- Reluctant to talk about finances because money is a taboo subject.
- You may fear that talking about money will make you vulnerable.
- You may worry that talking about money will make someone feel bad.

It's easy to become bogged down in self-criticism, blaming ourselves for not managing our finances properly.

However, we must know how it affects our finances to make an informed decision. We must determine whether we need to alter our money story. Because we are the author of our destiny, we have the power to craft a conclusion for ourselves.

"Francine" is the source of the following story.

In the middle of a session, Francine realized that her fear of success and money was connected to her money story. Now, instead of blaming circumstances, she realized that she was the one standing in her way of progress.

Francine recognized that her lack of action was her responsibility and sent her straight back into her old storyline of financial insecurity. Finally, she took ownership of being in control of this story.

Francine grew up in a home that struggled with money issues. After her father departed from the family while she was a child, he subsequently became semi-wealthy. Francine's mother was bitter, blaming his money and her lack of it for much of the family's hardships. He supplied nothing to the family. Francine's mother often chastised her for going "beyond her station" whenever she tried to improve herself.

THE MONEY BELIEF FORMULA: MINDSET + BEHAVIOR =...

Based on this old story, Francine told herself she was unworthy of success and money. She was convinced that money would make her a bad person, which led her to repeatedly destroy her success. For example, she turned away an opportunity to advance her career at a graphic design firm in lieu of a low-paying teaching post. In the the more recent stages of Francine's life, she was even undermining her own business.

Francine authored a new story, and it reads, "I am a successful businesswoman. I work very hard to build a business that supports my family and our dreams. I deserve to be successful, and I have earned every penny. I have clear plans for how I will use my finances to help my family reach our goals and give our children opportunities that we never had."

She continues to struggle with her resistance to larger successes in her company but feels stronger when she faces them from her new identity, as it takes over more with each passing day."

The more you connect with your money story, the more financially healthy you will become.

Your Return On Time Invested: Money Mindset

Do you want to feel confident in your financial decision-making and ability to make informed decisions for yourself?

You are entitled to the peace of mind that comes with financial freedom. The life you've built is one worth living. With the careful planning and hard work put into your financial independence, it's only right that you enjoy all of its benefits with no restrictions on how much money can be saved or made!

Your money story is an important entry point into a new narrative because it affects and influences many aspects of your life. If you can modify your money story, you will have made effective changes in your LIFE story.

How to begin writing a new chapter: Applying the AAA Principles of Change: Awareness. Acceptance. Action.

THE MONEY BELIEF FORMULA: MINDSET + BEHAVIOR =...

I want you to think (and write down) about what you heard, saw, thought, and felt, not just what you were told. I want you to think about yourself. Don't stifle your creativity. When you analyze the following questions, whatever bubbles to the top is very likely the truth:

- What was your family's attitude toward money like while growing up?
- How did you feel about spending money?
- What were your thoughts on saving money?
- What was your reaction to giving money away?
- What is your earliest financial memory?

- What financial messages did your mother instill in you? (Note: messages are distinct from lessons such as how to balance a checkbook.)
- What financial messages did your father pass along to you?
- Do you recall hearing your parents discuss (or argue about) money?
- Did you have more/less/about the same as your peers when growing up?

I've created a DIY Money Story Guide to help you apply the AAA principles of change. The good news is, it's possible to make a new story for how you approach your finances, and this tool will help guide you in doing so!

I invite you to make a date with your favorite people to dig into this essential question together: How can we unearth and change our money stories to win with wealth and achieve our best life?

Access download here https://www.herfinanceclub.com/1- DIY MS Guide

or scan the QR Code below.

THE MONEY BELIEF FORMULA: MINDSET + BEHAVIOR =...

This is very important because you are identifying a point where you change the story of your money mindset. You choose to move in a new direction and create a future of intentional money and greater abundance.

When you complete your Money Story Guide, you'll be two steps ahead of where most women start when it comes to building effective money beliefs. You won't just learn how to make a shield around your cash flow; you'll develop confidence and skills with every step that will get you closer to living the life you want through smart financial choices.

MY NOTES

MY NOTES

"Money, like emotions, is something you must control to keep your life on the right track."

— Natasha Munson

Chapter Four

Money Belief Formula for Living a Rich Life Now!

The money-believe formula is based on the idea that prosperity is a frame of mind, not necessarily a matter of luck or circumstances. As with anything else, it includes components like self-talk (self-starters for success), attitudes to promote success, and strategies to follow in life.

When you alter your money beliefs and rewire your brain you take the proper actions because you have the right beliefs.

Training your brain to be positive is no different from training your muscles at the gym. Recent research on neuroplasticity—the ability of the brain to change even in adulthood—reveals that as you develop new habits, you rewire the brain.

This chapter is about how the money-belief formula can be used to initiate a road map to financial well-being and begin working on specific steps toward building wealth now! Key elements of this formula include understanding:

- Money is like water-it flows toward where we place our attention most often.
- Money in the physical world is an energy system that flows from internal emotions to external results.
- Money is a mirror to reflect our feelings and beliefs about ourselves, others, and life in general!
- Money as an emotional system means that we respond to money emotionally; it can make us feel happy, sad, scared, or anxious. Money's not the enemy-it's how we think (feel) about money that makes all the difference in how much we have.
- Money as an energy system means that we can attract everything into our life-money included-by the way we think (feel) and act toward it.

THE MONEY BELIEF FORMULA: MINDSET + BEHAVIOR =...

- Mastering our belief formula for living the life we want now is a belief system that will help us see ourselves as a money magnet, attract money into our life on purpose, and use the money to make the changes in our life that will bring us what we want!

Being a smart woman requires us to master the money-mindset formula. Then, our positive thinking and financial well-being can be translated into healthy behaviors with money.

Three parts are critical for our financial success. Part One: Build a Strong Financial Foundation, Part Two: Money Management, and Part Three: Wealth Building.

We have covered the first part of starting to build a strong financial foundation, our money mindset, in this book and bridging the gap between the two key issues that most people and the financial industry overlook:

- How we value money and our "Money-story" and
- How we relate to money.

Please know no one ever consistently achieved their financial goals, no matter how good their money system and wealth growth knowledge, without first acknowledging and connecting to their relationship with their money.

When it comes to being your Wealthiest Self:

To achieve our wealthiest self, I like to use the old three-legged stool analogy as a clever way to demonstrate that stability and confidence are dependent on all of your assets, not just one. This is why this system assists women in recognizing their beliefs, where they are heading, and how they can change them to achieve better results in the future. Moreover, it is a set of habits that will help you win the most important game of your life: wealth creation.

Mmm hmmm. Do you know what they say about consistency, I hear you ask? Well, okay then! The truth of it (and this sounds like common sense, but sometimes we need reminding) - It's important in life; because if something goes wrong or changes quickly around us, how will our resolve stand up against them?? And so forth, etc.

For this, I leave you with the following actions that will help you transform your relationship with money into a more positive and healthy one:

Give money a new meaning

THE MONEY BELIEF FORMULA: MINDSET + BEHAVIOR =...

Find alternative terms for debt and obligations and call it whatever you want. Consider that your rent or mortgage, phone bill, car payment contribute to a higher quality of life, so there is no point in viewing them as a burden.

This psychological trick will allow you to personalize how you use money and transform its negative connotation into a more positive attitude and, of course, outcome.

Create a knowledge bank

Make time every day to learn something new about money.

It only takes a minute or two, and even if it's just skimming through the business headlines in the newspaper or glancing at money blogs, it brings new ideas to mind and keeps finances on our radar screen.

It's difficult to understand money if we don't understand the terminology or the current trends. Listen to a podcast while driving or watch TV shows or YouTube channels with people discussing money while cooking dinner.

Encourage a spirit of abundance.

Consider doing something relaxing like meditating or walking when you're stressed about money or don't have enough of it.

De-stressing can help us develop actionable steps to either increase our income or solve our money problems.

The key to implementing most of this knowledge and exercises is to be consistent and persistent in building a strong, positive, and healthy Money mindset that adapts to your personal needs and goals.

This concept also forces us to reconsider our interpretations of success and wealth. The word "success" can mean different things to different people. That is, there are numerous ways to earn money. Some people require a large sum of money, while others require a small sum. Some people have more money than others. And some people will always be more willing to take risks than others.

Trusting in our process and our financial wealth path will provide us with the keys to discovering our "point of equilibrium" between our success and financial wealth.

Make sure you're giving yourself the help you need

While it's nice to think we can handle money on our own, the truth is that most of us need support from others. We tend to hold back and not ask for help when we should be reaching out more often.

THE MONEY BELIEF FORMULA: MINDSET + BEHAVIOR =...

Whether we're looking for guidance or want someone there to listen while we figure things out, do not go at this alone! A good place to start is women's money groups such as the Herfinance Club, a private Facebook group.

Organizing a study session with friends or a financial book club is an effective way to learn more about wealth creation and self-sabotage (when fear rears its ugly head).

If you're having trouble overcoming your limiting beliefs on your own, you could benefit from the help of a Financial Coach/Money Coach or Financial Therapist.

Make sure you're giving yourself the help you need. You don't need to know and do everything on your own.

Getting help can be the single most powerful and bravest thing we can do at times.

The following are some questions to ask a potential money coach:

- Do you also handle individuals' financial behavior as well as personal finance issues?
- What if, as we work together, I become stressed, nervous, or frustrated? Do you allow for the emotional part of the money, too?

- Do you have any experience with or therapy training? What kind of financial experience do you have?

It is important to find the best fit for you personally. You should not follow a one-size-fits-all philosophy regarding debt, savings, or other money areas because every person has different needs!

If you're ready to take your relationship with money to the next level, I'm here to help. Let me share my personal experience and expertise on how you can get more out of life by mastering your finances.

You are invited to join me for an exclusive full financial initiation coaching program to help you create a new mindset around money. It doesn't have power over you anymore! I'll show you exactly what steps need to be taken to break free from old patterns and make conscious choices about where your money goes every day. This step towards getting clarity around what matters most will allow you the freedom and confidence necessary to live a fulfilling life on YOUR terms!

Join me today - click link 1-1 Tailored Premier Program "Take Control of Your Money" or scan QR Code.

THE MONEY BELIEF FORMULA: MINDSET + BEHAVIOR =...

Your Return On-time Invested: Money Belief Formula.

Three exercises to connect with your wealth

Abundance and wealth are states of mind. Abundance is the belief and confidence that everything we require is already within us and that our task is to perform that inner search to access that inner wealth and prosperity. It is a state of endless gratitude.

Abundance does not only have to do with monetary issues. It is related to all those blessings that you possess. You can have an abundance of love, of opportunities, of good times, of food. That is to say that even without money, you can be and enjoy a wonderful state of abundance. Start by recognizing it.

I share these three simple and easy exercises to generate abundance and wealth. The recommendation is that you practice one activity every day.

Wealth Exercise #1: Call inspirational people in your life

THE MONEY BELIEF FORMULA: MINDSET + BEHAVIOR =...

Who are the people who inspire you the most, who would you like to be "when you grow up"?

Think of one person in particular that you are inspired by right now.

Someone who has overcome their initial struggles and struck gold from them. A person you admire and aspire to follow in their footsteps.

Say their name out loud right now. "------."

For just 60 seconds, imagine they're in the room with you, and then express your admiration and desire to be like them, your gratitude for their inspiration, wisdom, guidance, and encouragement that they have given you just by being who they are.

Wealth exercise #2: Enjoy all the prosperity you see

Which reaction do you have if you see a high-end car, luxurious home or boat or vast estate, or other signs of wealth? Bitterness and negativity toward OTHERS' riches is almost always a barrier to achieving it, and even if you do, you will not be able to appreciate it fully.

Whenever you see a material thing or sign of wealth, do the 60-second wealth exercise and CONGRATULATE THEIR OWNERS. Whether you know them or not is immaterial; all you have to do is say things like, "Well done, owner of this house!"

Making an effort to enjoy the prosperity you see or feel will be easier when you do this.

Well done, keep repeating that to yourself. It's a fantastic house! One day, I hope to own a place similar to that! Alternatively, think and say kind things about it.

This communicates to our subconscious mind what we hope to achieve in life and WHERE WE DREAM OF BEING.

Wealth Exercise #3: Think about what you have to be grateful for

Today you will do something easy and very enjoyable.

Sit in silence, close your eyes, and simply think of three things you are grateful for, here and now. Take a deep breath as you list and give thanks for each of these things and then write them in your journal.

THE MONEY BELIEF FORMULA: MINDSET + BEHAVIOR =...

This can be as simple as "my eyesight" or "a computer I can read my email on," or as profound as "my soul" or "a bright new morning full of wonders yet to come."

If you want to express gratitude, it doesn't matter how big or small the thing you're grateful for is.

Gratitude is the starting point for your abundance mindset. If you want to develop healthy money habits, you must learn to appreciate what you already have and not just work hard for more things.

MY NOTES

MY NOTES

"Without leaps of imagination or dreaming, we lose the excitement of possibilities. Dreaming, after all, is a form of planning."

— Gloria Steinem

Chapter Five

Powerful Affirmations to Luck Into a Richer Soul and Happier Mindset

Attracting wealth is extremely simple if we have the right tools. We only need two words, "I Am." With these two simple words, we can form Prosperity Phrases.

Our mind is a magnet that attracts everything it thinks, good or bad. That is why we must focus on these Positive Phrases to Attract Abundance and Prosperity to our life.

SUSAN M. DIAMOND

These Positive Phrases, Prosperity Decrees, or simply Abundance Mantras, are the key to our success on autopilot.

To change our minds for the better and achieve prosperity, we must repeat these phrases throughout our day as often as possible. Only through repetition will we be able to change our minds positively.

It takes 21 to 66 days to install a habit, so do not hesitate to put into practice all the exercises that I have left you so far for at least 30 days in a row to change your life.

We don't need to be fully conscious of what we are saying. We can repeat it while working, at night, while relaxing or while exercising.

With this simple technique, our life will be filled with abundance and prosperity automatically. These prosperity affirmations will attract a lot into our life.

- I have the power to manifest abundance in every area of my life," and "My mind is powerful enough to overcome all fear.
- I am smart enough to overcome all financial fears. I am a person full of abundance, wealth, and prosperity.

THE MONEY BELIEF FORMULA: MINDSET + BEHAVIOR =...

- I am a magnetic person. I attract interesting people into my life who appreciate me and encourage me to progress.
- I am a person full of abundance, wealth, and prosperity.
- I am a successful person. My projects work perfectly, and all my plans go in the direction I want them to go.
- My affirmations work for me, and I attract everything I think about.
- Having the life I want is simple. It's just a matter of picturing it in my mind, and I attract everything I think about. My mind is a magnet.
- I inevitably attract success. It comes to me all the time, and I welcome it with open arms.
- I am the definition of success.
- It is inevitable for me to smile. I have happiness stamped on my face, and I notice it every morning when I wake up and look in the mirror. I see absolute bliss.
- I have the life I want, and my dreams are a reality.
- Money comes to me in a landslide. It comes into my life in huge amounts and continuously because I deserve it. I earn the money that comes to me because of the value I bring to the lives of others.

- I am a person who brings value to others and is happy to give.
- I am a person who shares my abundance because prosperity comes to me in a flowing way.
- I am an amazing person. I move through the world with confidence because I believe in myself. And because I believe in me, others believe in me.
- The world is abundant, and I am a part of it.
- Money comes into my life in huge amounts, and I accept it happily because I know I deserve it.
- I have thoughts of prosperity.
- I am a person who accomplishes my goals easily and quickly because I am focused.
- I give prosperity to everyone who comes my way. I am a success.
- When I wake up in the morning, I look in the mirror, and I see only success.
- I have full confidence in myself, my abilities, and my decisions.
- I love to make decisions. I am an action taker. So for me making decisions is a no-brainer.
- I am a person who loves to step out of my comfort zone. I am comfortable taking my life to the fullest.
- Every day is a window of opportunity that appears before me.
- Wealth is simply something that happens in my life.

THE MONEY BELIEF FORMULA: MINDSET + BEHAVIOR =...

- Luck is always with me. I am a lucky person to whom everything goes as planned.
- I attract everything I think about, and since I am abundant, I draw prosperity, wealth, and love.
- I like to work on myself. I take care of my body and mind. As a result, I develop all my physical, mental, and spiritual potential.
- I love to work on myself. I am a person who aligns with the good life and always moves forward.
- I surround myself with abundant people who appreciate me, and I appreciate them.
- I am prosperous; an endless stream of wealth flows in me.
- Money comes to me without limit.
- I accept prosperity and abundance in my life.
- I am the best version of myself.
- I am unique.
- I take charge of my financial life and stand up for my own needs and desires.
- I am amazing, and my actions reflect how amazing I am.
- I let my highest self make my financial decisions. I make choices from a place of joy, wisdom, and freedom.
- I attract everything I think about and only think positive thoughts.

- I create abundance in my mind, and with just thought, it comes into my life.
- I have fun with the people I love. I live around interesting people and attract successful people into my life.
- Talking to people is easy for me. Conversations flow, and I always have fun talking to people. It adds value to their lives.
- I have friends who love me, and I love them.
- I share my abundance and am always the first to help others.
- I feel success flowing through my body. I can feel it coursing through my whole being and staying with me. Success is in me. I am a success.
- I am the creator of my success.
- My life is pure success.

Your Return On-time Invested: Money Affirmations.

Affirmations are a powerful tool to reprogram all those toxic money beliefs that prevent us from achieving our professional and financial success.

This happens because new commands help us integrate new thoughts about prosperity and money consciously and unconsciously; we can break those habits and toxic beliefs that sabotage us and prevent us from achieving what we want.

As I mentioned in the chapter we just finished reading, we need to be very consistent with repetition because it takes us at least a month to integrate new ideas into our minds.

As a result, because I know that repeating positive affirmations can be difficult for beginners, here are two new exercises to help you transition into daily affirmation practice.

Positive affirmations: two ways to make them easier

Integrate positive affirmations into your daily routine with the help of these simple tips, so you can begin to lay the foundation for your wealth and abundance.

Tip #1: Record your affirmations

A better understanding of positive affirmations and how to use them is now in your hands. So choose your favorite or even create your own and record them using your mobile apps so that you can listen to them at any time of the day or night, as desired.

I recommend that you start the day in the best way by listening to your positive affirmations and end the day listening to them again so that they can be definitively integrated into your subconscious.

You can also take advantage of lunchtime, gym workout, jogging time, or perhaps your work routine to listen to yourself repeating your affirmations, which will guarantee excellent results.

Tip #2: Vision Board

THE MONEY BELIEF FORMULA: MINDSET + BEHAVIOR =...

The Vision Board is a popular tool to visualize our positive affirmations and goals in a fun, easy, and daily way.

Visualization of what we want to achieve is the best motivation. It is also a distraction from stress by showing a light at the end of the tunnel.

The reason we stay motivated is that we'll always be getting the best possible result.

Vision boards have simple psychology, but many people who use them believe they are more than just a piece of art and work like magic.

Let's get started!

- The most common way to create a vision board is to use a collage on cardboard or design on the computer.
- Spend some time contemplating your objectives. Embrace your imagination and let yourself be swept away.
- Seek out visuals that motivate and inspire you. Images can be drawn, printed from the internet, or torn from magazines.
- Include words and affirmations that are supportive of your goal. You can either print them or handwrite them.

- Don't just think about things in terms of their functionality; also consider how they make you feel. For example, in what way will it make you feel when you finally pay off all your debt?
- Arrange and adhere them to your flip file or board now. Then, let your creativity run wild as you play with your vision board's embellishments.

Your vision board should be placed somewhere where you can see it every day and remind you of the outcome that you're working toward.

You can see this every time you wake up and go to sleep, start your days on the right foot, and program yourself to receive all the abundance that the world wants to give you.

MY NOTES

Appreciation Message:

Thanks for reading, and if you enjoyed the book, please consider leaving an honest review on Amazon so that I can continue to write books that help women on their financial journeys!

>> Click here to leave a quick review

I would be extremely grateful if you could take sixty seconds to leave a brief review on Amazon, even if it's only a few sentences: https://amzn.to/3j9x3k7

"Today is the first day of the rest of your life."

— Anonymous

Conclusion

I know that you want to improve your relationship with money by bringing more balance and harmony into the equation. And to accomplish this, you need to be excited and hopeful about your financial future.

That means you must overcome any feelings of scarcity, such as not being good enough, not feeling good enough, or not having enough, as these can lead to stress and anxiety.

I realize that life is far too short to be worrying about our future, but the good news is that there is a process that can assist us in achieving our desired wealth.

Getting rid of the money blocks and limiting beliefs about success is an important part of this process, which is nothing more than our subconscious system of self-sabotage to prevent us from achieving the wealth we deserve. It takes three steps to become conscious of what is going on and to go beyond it:

> 1. Uncover Your Money Story - Result - The more you connect to your money story, the more financially healthy you will become.
> 2. Translate Money Meanings - Result - Conquer your money mindset and take control of your finances.
> 3. Rewire for wealth - Result - Transform your habits and win with wealth for you and your family.

Having personal and financial success is not only attainable; it's already a part of our DNA.

Growing up, you may have been taught or experienced seeing the world through the lens of scarcity by your parents and teachers, but that doesn't have to be the case in your present or future life.

The only person who can make a positive difference in your current situation is YOU. You can only begin to change your limiting beliefs about money by committing to a daily practice of kindness, self-love, recognition, and prosperity. It would help if you did this from a personal place and consciousness to begin replacing your limiting

THE MONEY BELIEF FORMULA: MINDSET + BEHAVIOR =...

beliefs about money, such as your fear of success and financial prosperity.

The path to winning your money game also includes developing a new financial roadmap for adopting healthier money behaviors such as positive and sustainable spending, saving, generating passive income streams, and investing.

You can also start laying the foundation to reclaim your natural wealth successfully and practice good health and wellness habits that nourish your emotional and physical well-being. One of the tips that I have lovingly put together for you is to use gratitude as a daily tool to make yourself aware of existing abundance and start building a path of wealth, success, and prosperity.

Of course, the real magic happens once you put these steps into action. Practicing them daily and including them into your daily routine will guarantee positive results in a few weeks if you are willing to put in the effort and energy that your money path deserves.

Remember that it will take you at least a month of consistent practice to internalize these new positive money beliefs and ideas and begin noticing positive shifts in your relationship with money, people, and prosperity.

SUSAN M. DIAMOND

Even so, I understand that a challenge like this can be difficult to follow, or perhaps it's very difficult to see what might be preventing you from progressing because you're so close to it.

We connected for a reason.

You got here because you needed to be here.

So here's what I'd like to do for you.

SCAN the QR code to set up a quick call.

I'd love to offer you our Wealth Foundation Assessment, it is completely free of charge and a great first step toward helping you discover where your financial foundation is weakest. In order to change your money story and/or open up new avenues for wealth creation, this diagnostic

THE MONEY BELIEF FORMULA: MINDSET + BEHAVIOR =...

will show you exactly where your attention should be directed first.

With this information, you will be able to improve your financial outcomes and start winning with wealth.

And if you want my support in doing that, I'll share some ways to help you.

But first, you need to stop pausing your big day. You need to stop finding new pretexts, postponing the call, exercises, or the solution.

Convince yourself that finally, your natural wealth is coming back to you in the form of this book and my guidance, and let's find the way to navigate through your fears, doubts, and the phantoms of your negative money beliefs and put them very far away from this fresh start.

Why?

Because when we're afraid of something - whether it's spiders or bills - our power over those things is limited because they tie us up in knots with anxiety every time there's another chance for trouble; but when we know what needs to be done but aren't afraid to try new things instead, well, let me tell you: That feels pretty good no matter how old YOU get!!

SUSAN M. DIAMOND

So, do yourself a huge favor and begin today to alter your perspective on money and the benefits it can provide you.

Changing your money mindset does not happen overnight. But, if you can get past the fear, I truly believe it will be a necessary first step in improving one's financial situation and will lead you on your way to achieving any goal you desire!

Resources

Avila, T. (n.d.). 20 Money Mantras To Inspire Financial Freedom. https://bit.ly/3iZW1SY

Bergland , C. (2015). The Neuroscience Of Making a Decision. Psychology Today. https://bit.ly/Berglandc

Chatsky, J. (2019). Women With Money. New York: Grand Central Publishing.

Clason, G. (2011). The Richest Man In Babylon. Oxford: Myriad Editions. First published in 1926 by Penguin (New York).

Corley, T. (2010). Rich Habits: The Daily Success Habits of Wealthy Individuals. Minneapolis: Langdon Street Press.

Curtis, J. (February 12, 2014). How Money Can Change People and Affect Their Behavior. https://bit.ly/3J41C5x

Diamond, S. (2021, April). Herfinance Club. About. https://www.herfinanceclub.com/about

Diamond, S. (March 8, 2022). Herfinance Talk on Apple Podcasts. Women and Wealth: Becoming Fearless. https://apple.co/3u2LGMt

Diamond, S. (2021, October 17). The Small Actions We Take That Add Up To Improve Personal Finance. https://bit.ly/37ar9N9

Domzalski, D. (2017, July 5). Run The Money: Fuel Your Financial Future | Budgeting Hacks | Make Money | Manage money. https://bit.ly/3wZJsPK

Dweck, C. (2006). Mindset: The Psychology of Success. New York: Random House.

Enotes.com. (n.d.). Shakespeare Quotes. https://bit.ly/3J58Ypf

Gerstley, A. F. (2018). The 30-Day Money Cleanse. Naperville, USA: Sourcebooks, Inc.

THE MONEY BELIEF FORMULA: MINDSET + BEHAVIOR =...

Hamm, T. (September 5, 2011). Money Is Not The Root Of All Evil. https://bit.ly/3K57pce

Honda, K. (2019, May 29). Let Go Of Your Negative Beliefs About Money. https://bit.ly/3K4EG7r

Hurst, K. (2021, August 19). How To Attract Money And Wealth With The Law Of Attraction-. https://bit.ly/3x0QvYG

Huson, B. (2021). Rewire for wealth: Three Steps Any Woman Can Take to Program Her Brain for Financial Success. New York: McGraw - Hill Education.

Ilivethelifellove.com. (n.d.). Six Exercises To Attract Money Now. https://bit.ly/3u0a4yk

Kiyosaki, R. (2017). Rich Dad Poor Dad: What the Rich Teach Their Kids About Money That the Poor and Middle Class Do Not. Scottsdale: Plata Publishing.

Klaric, J. (2019). Connect With Money. Spain: Plant Publishing

Krueger, D. (2019). Your New Money Story The Beliefs, Behaviors, And Brain Science To Rewire for Wealth. New York: Rowman & Littlefield.

Munson, N. (2005). Life Lessons for My Sisters: How to Make Wise Choices and Live a Life You Love! Paris: Hachette Books.

Numerologymasters.co. (2021, October 11). 369 Manifestation Method. https://bit.ly/3iZDjuJ

Rochard, M. (2020). Personal Finance QuickStart Guide: The Simplified Beginner's Guide to Eliminating Financial Stress, Building Wealth, and Achieving Financial Freedom. Albany, USA: ClydeBank Media

Samso, R. (2019). The Money Code: Free, wise and rich. https://amzn.to/3u49Oy4

Sokunbi, B. (2019). Clever Girl Finance: Ditch Debt, Save Money And Build Real Wealth. Hoboken, USA: Wiley.

Wong, K. (September 8, 2016). Money Is Not Your Enemy or a Goal; It's a Tool. https://bit.ly/3j1HpT2

About The Author

Susan Diamond, MSW, is a Certified Financial Social Worker, aka Money Coach, Podcast Host, and Founder of The Herfinance Club, where she helps women improve their money mindset and confidence so they can reduce stress, release shame, regain control and unleash and balance their financial power.

Her mission is to spread the message that it's okay for women to talk money because knowledge is power, and when that knowledge helps you become more independent, it leads to empowerment.

SUSAN M. DIAMOND

Her goal is to inspire ONE MILLION women to start the money conversation and move past the taboos and hang-ups about talking about money and finances to help take steps to put themselves in a better situation than they were in before.

She began her career in finance not as an economist or a financial planner, but as a social worker interested in people's attitudes and emotional reactions to money. She loves exploring the complexities of women's relationships with money and helping them uncover their "money story" to help them transform their financial future.

For more resources, go to www.Herfinanceclub.com or scan QR code

Join Herfinanceclub private Facebook group

THE MONEY BELIEF FORMULA: MINDSET + BEHAVIOR =...

Follow on Instagram @herfinanceclub

Subscribe to Podcast

Made in the USA
Middletown, DE
25 April 2022

64593824R00071